FUN WITH FINGER PAINTING

MOONSTONE

How To Use This Book

Press your thumb down on the paint and the press it down on the paper.

Press the tip of your index finger down on the paint and press it down on the paper.

Or just use the very tip of your fingers and thumbs!

Tools & Materials

All you need is your hand, paint and pencils / colour pencils to get started.

Follow the simple steps to create each picture. Use markers or crayons to complete each picture.

Angel

1

2

3

4

5

6

Rabbit

1

2

3

4

5

6

Caterpiller

1

2

3

4

5

6

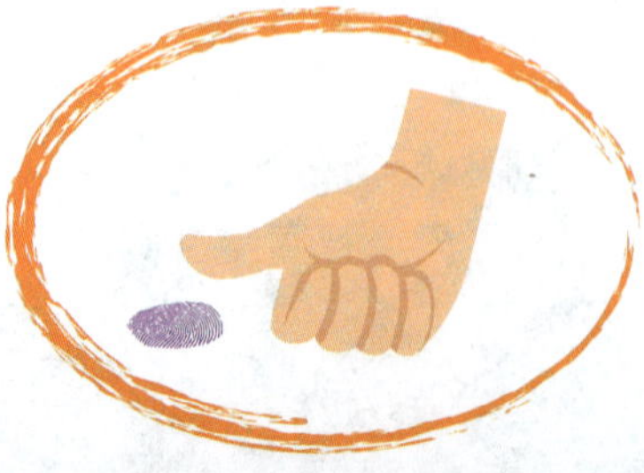

Flower

Dragonfly

1

2

3

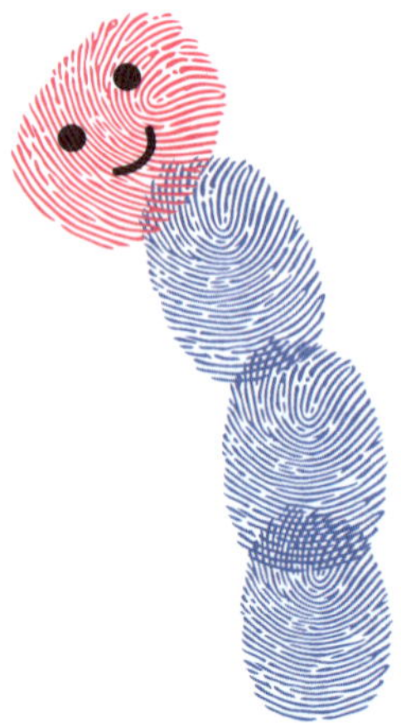

4

5

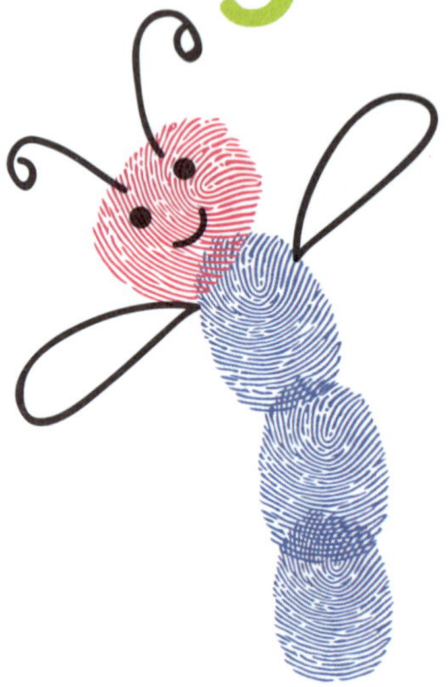

6

Peacock

1

2

3

4

Reindeer

1

2

3

4

Lion

1

2

3

4

5

6

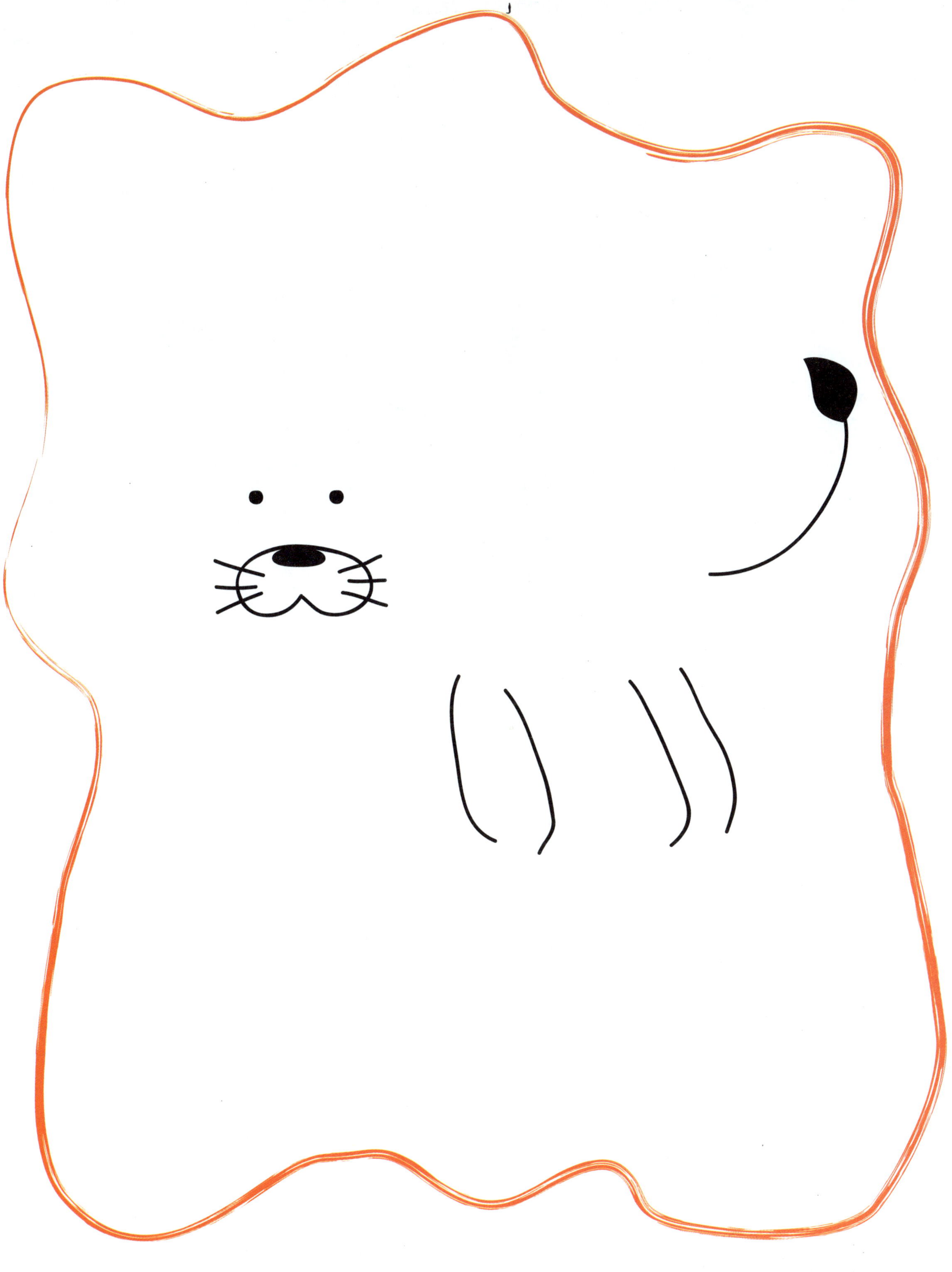

Koala

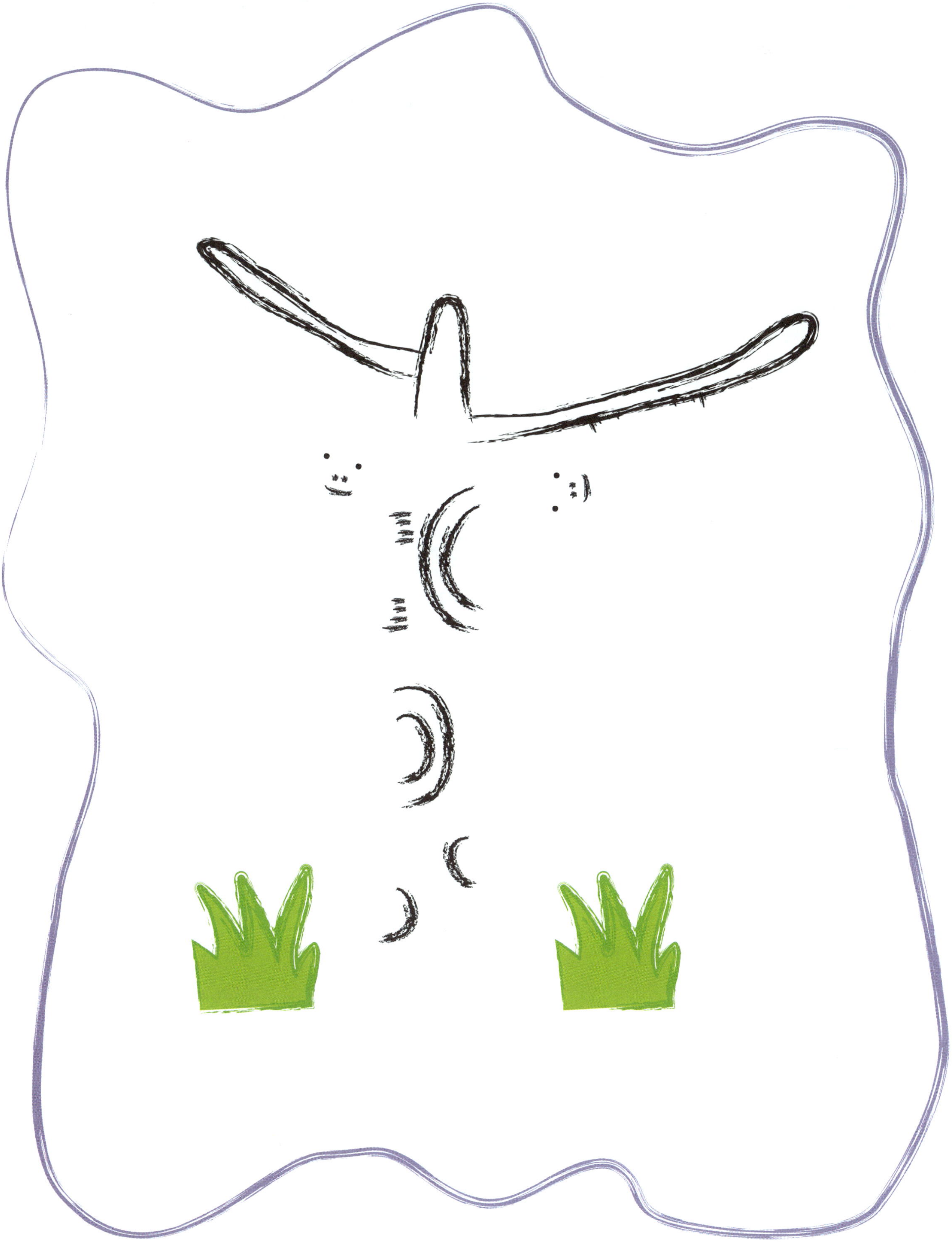

Princess

1

2

3

4

5

6

Kangaroo

1

2

3

4

5

6

Birthday Party

Fish

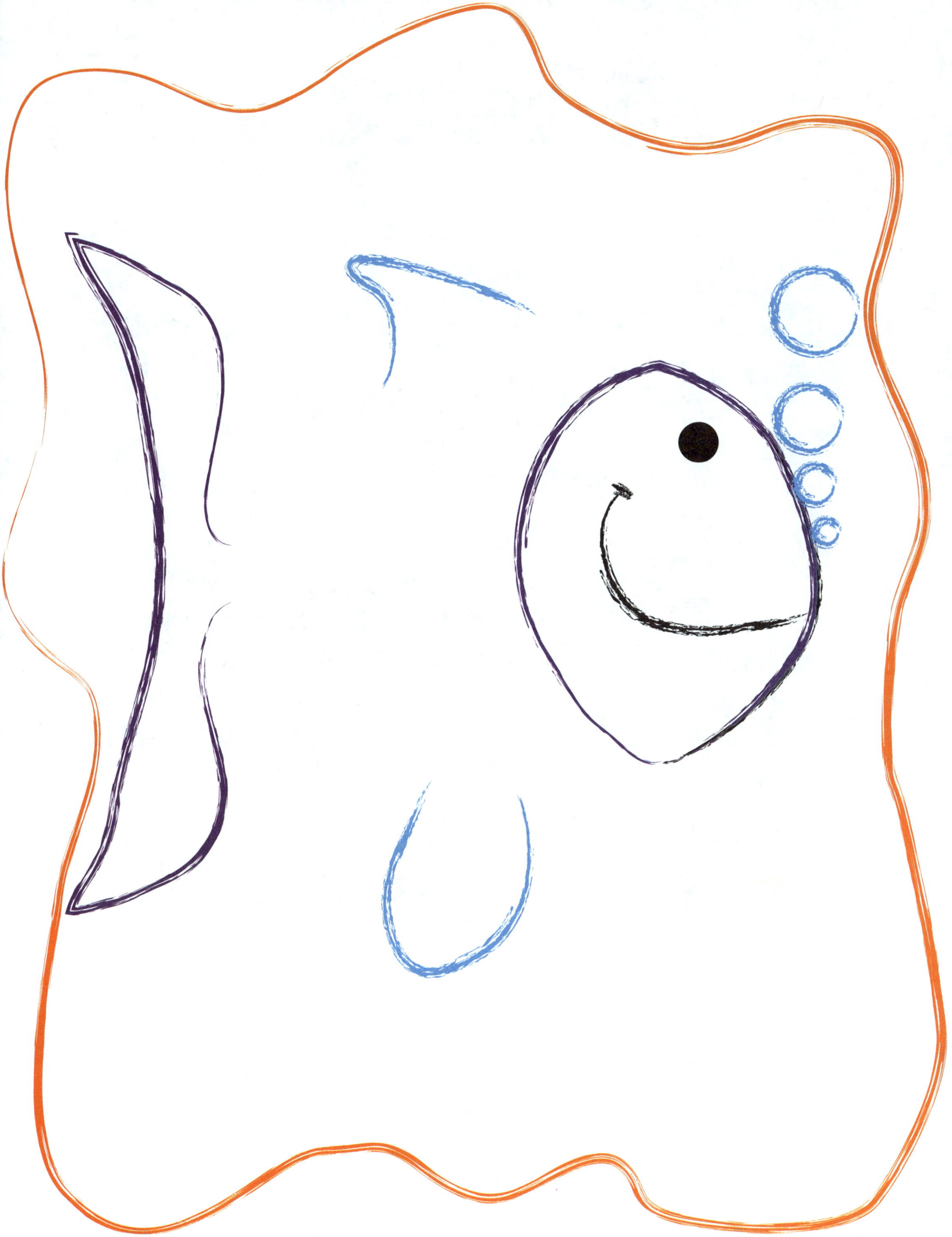

Sheep

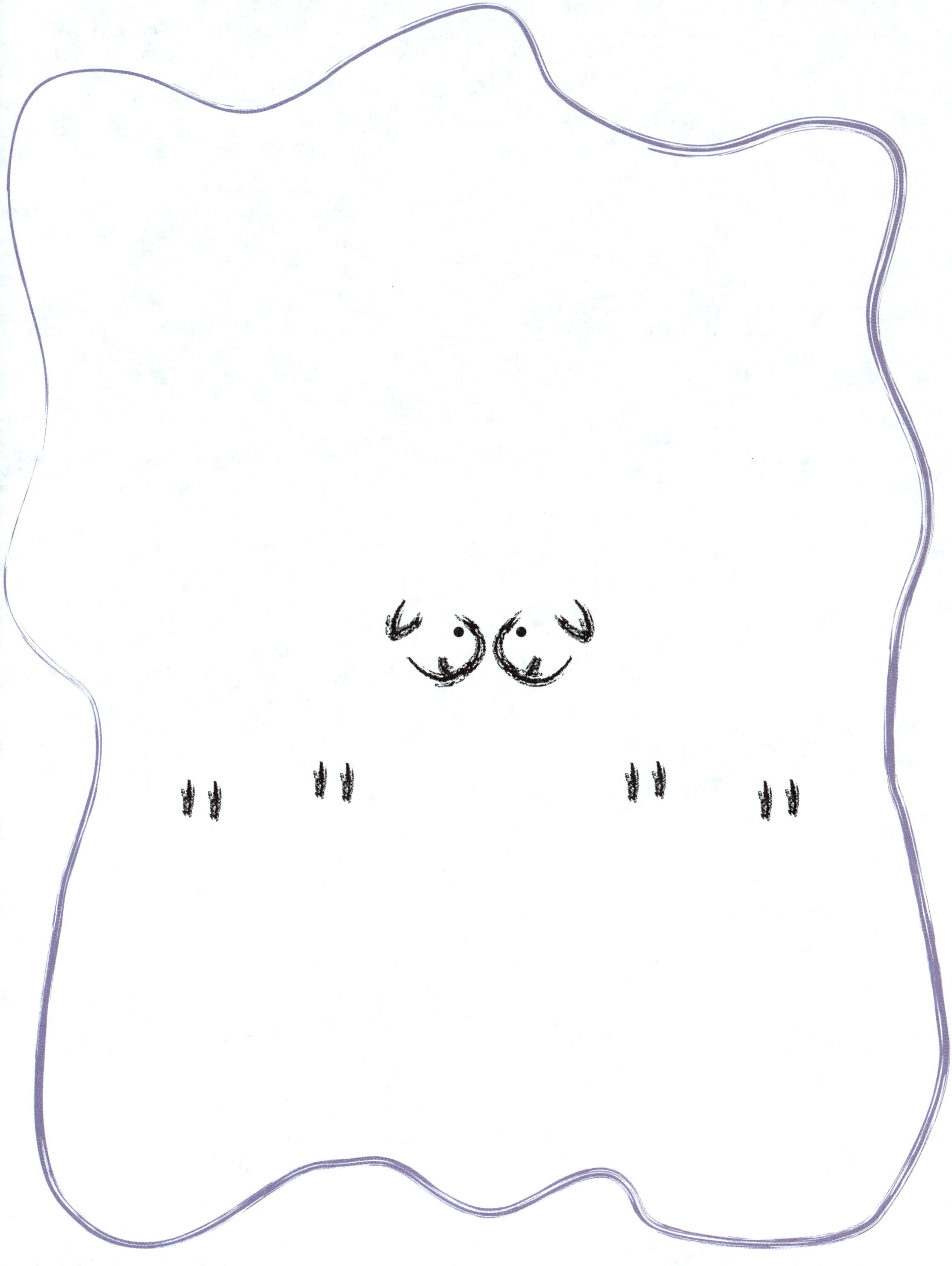